Towers Reach High

Towers Reach High

a building block book

Lee Sullivan Hill

Carolrhoda Books, Inc./Minneapolis

For my mother—L. S. H.

For metric conversion, when you know the number of feet, multiply by 0.30 to find the number of meters.

Photographs reproduced through the courtesy of : Thomas D. Parker, front cover; Dick Hemingway, back cover, p. 1; Elizabeth Buie, p. 2; Frank S. Balthis, pp. 5, 24; Russell Adams, p. 6; Thomas Mark Szelog, pp. 7, 11, 13; Paul T. McMahon, p. 8; Jerry Hennen, p. 9; Thomas R. Fletcher, pp. 10, 25; Eliot Cohen, p. 12; Dr. Donald Poulton, p. 14; Michele Burgess, pp. 15, 28; Howard Ande, pp. 16, 17, 22; Kay Shaw, p. 18; Myrtis & Brack Olds, Olds Illustrative Photography, p. 19; Karlene V. Schwartz, p. 20; Jo-ann Ordano, pp. 21, 29; Galyn C. Hammond, p. 23; Cheryl Koenig Morgan, p. 26; James P. Rowan, p. 27.

Carolrhoda Books, Inc. c/o The Lerner Group
241 First Avenue North, Minneapolis, MN 55401

Library of Congress Cataloging-in-Publication Data

Hill, Lee Sullivan, 1958–
    Towers reach high / by Lee Sullivan Hill.
        p.   cm. — (A building block book)
    Includes index.
    Summary: An introduction to the variety and beauty of towers, including the purposes they serve.
        ISBN 1-57505-036-6
        1. Towers—Design and construction—Juvenile literature. [1. Towers] I. Title.
    II. Series: Hill, Lee Sullivan, 1958—Building block book.
    TA660.T6H55   1997
    725'.97—DC20   96-22109

Manufactured in the United States of America
1 2 3 4 5 6 SP 02 01 00 99 98 97

Towers are tall. They reach high, up to the sky.
When you stand beside a tower, you have to tilt
your head way back to see the top.

Some towers have strange shapes. Many churches in Russia have domes shaped like candy kisses. The towers at Saint Basil's Cathedral swirl with color.

These towers can move. Cranes load cargo
onto a ship. Bundles of logs swing through the
air with ease.

Take an elevator to the top of the Sears Tower. It has 110 stories of glass and steel. When the elevator stops, you feel light for a second, as if you might keep going.

Tall towers help people see into the
distance. Look out from the top of the Tower
of the Americas. The city sparkles below.

You can see far down the coast of Puerto Rico
from this old tower. Soldiers kept watch for
enemies from its windows. Do you think they
stayed up all night?

Forest rangers watch for an enemy, too. Fire! They climb up into a tower and watch the forest. If they see smoke, they radio firefighters right away.

Towers can help us find our way. An airport
tower stands tall beside the runway. Workers
inside help pilots take off and land safely.

A lighthouse guides ships around rocks and sandbars. The shining light warns the captain to steer clear of trouble.

Some towers send messages. They broadcast television and radio shows. If you lived near Toronto, your Saturday morning cartoons might be broadcast from the CN Tower.

The Eiffel Tower is a broadcast tower, too. But most people think it's just for fun. Elevators go up and down the legs of the tower. You can see all of Paris from the top.

Some towers hold things. A silo stores feed
for cows. The cows eat after they are milked.

Great, tall grain elevators store corn and wheat grown by farmers. The grain pours out like water. It is loaded on trains and sent around the world.

Water towers store water. Stone and brick made old water towers strong. Have you ever picked up a full bucket? Water is heavy!

Strong steel holds water in newer towers.
Steel can be shaped and painted many ways.
It can even look like fruit.

Some towers work hard for a living. A windmill catches the wind. It turns wind into power.

A team of windmills can make lots of power.
This wind farm makes enough electricity to light
a whole town.

Some towers inspire instead of work. The towers on churches are called spires. (It even sounds like *inspire*.) Country churches have simple spires.

Mosques have needle-like towers called minarets. The Mosque of Sultan Hasan was built more than six hundred years ago.

The Seattle Space Needle was built in 1962. The people of Seattle wanted to show what the future might be like. What do you think a tower of the future will look like?

The builders of the Washington Monument wanted to remember the past. Go up the stone steps, around and around. When you reach the top, look out the windows. Pink cherry blossoms float far below.

You can build a tower just for fun. Pancake towers are tasty with maple syrup dripping off the top. Or build a block tower. Careful it doesn't fall!

When you grow up, you could build a tower out of steel and concrete. You could be a forest ranger and watch for fires from a tower. You could even run a crane and swing logs up in the air.

Towers come in many shapes and sizes. They do work and they inspire. Sometimes they just make us stare up in wonder.

Towers reach for the sky.

A Photo Index to the Towers in This Book

 **Cover** Alexandre Gustave Eiffel designed the Eiffel Tower to show how iron could be used for buildings. The iron tower amazed visitors to the Paris World's Fair in 1889.

 **Page 1** The Daymark warns captains to keep their ships away from the rocky shore. It is a signal tower near Cornwall, England. Its bright red and white stripes stand out clearly during the day.

 **Page 2** You would have to climb 414 steps to reach the top of this bell tower in Florence, Italy. A famous architect named Giotto planned it more than 600 years ago.

 **Page 5** The sky reflects off a skyscraper in New York City. You would get a sore neck if you tried to look up at all the towers there.

 **Page 6** St. Basil's Cathedral was built in the 1500s by a Russian leader called Ivan the Terrible. It has been made into a historical museum.

 **Page 7** Cargo ships have cranes attached to their decks. The *Bonita* will carry logs from Maine to Turkey.

 **Page 8** The Sears Tower in Chicago, Illinois, was built in 1974. Inside, 104 elevator cabs zip up and down between the floors.

 **Page 9** The Tower of the Americas was built for HemisFair '68 in San Antonio, Texas. Two other towers in this book were built for a world's fair. Can you find them?

 **Page 10** Spanish soldiers watched for French and English warships from the tower of El Morro. The tower overlooks San Juan harbor in Puerto Rico. The remains of a Spanish fort lie below, at the water's edge.

 **Page 11** This fire tower stands tall in Molly Stark State Park in Vermont. Forest rangers used to spend all summer in their lookout watching for fires. The one room held a bed, a table and chair, maps, and a logbook.

Now equipment and airplanes help rangers find fires. The Forest Service rents some of the unused towers to campers (who are not afraid of heights).

Page 12 The antennae on the tower at Grenier Airport in Manchester, New Hampshire, look like hairs on a robot head.

Page 13 George Washington signed the order to build the Portland Head Light at Cape Elizabeth, Maine. The smaller lighthouse, called a ledge light, was added later. Both lights still guide ships into the harbor.

Page 14 The Canadian National (CN) Tower soars 1,815 feet into the sky above Toronto, Ontario. The round bump holds an observation deck and restaurant. Would you like to eat sitting 1,150 feet in the air?

Page 15 With its broadcast antennae, the Eiffel Tower stands 1,049 feet tall. It must be painted every seven years, with 50 tons of brown paint.

Page 16 Older silos, like the one on this dairy farm in Plato, Illinois, unload their corn through a hole at the top. Newer silos unload feed through a gate at the bottom.

Page 17 This grain elevator sticks up from the flat land west of Panhandle, Texas.

Page 18 The Eden Park Water Tower serves Cincinnati, Ohio. People learned a long time ago to store water up high. Then the water could flow downhill when needed.

Page 19 Gaffney, South Carolina, has a steel water tower. Builders chose a peach shape because many farmers in the area grow peaches. During the night, pumps push water uphill to fill the water tower. In the morning when everyone turns on the water to brush their teeth, the water runs down from the tower and out of the faucets.

Page 20 A steady breeze blows across the wide-open spaces of this dairy farm in Wisconsin. The wind turns the windmill, which pumps water up from a well.

 **Page 21** Thousands of wind turbines dot the Altamont Pass in California. Warm air rises from the valley below and turns the turbines to make electricity.

 **Page 22** The New Preston Congregational Church was built almost 200 years ago in Connecticut. Spires are also called steeples. This wooden steeple holds a bell that rings to call people to worship.

 **Page 23** The Mosque of Sultan Hasan is in Cairo, Egypt. It celebrates the religion of Islam. People climb to the top of the minarets to call worshipers together.

 **Page 24** The Seattle Space Needle was built for Century 21, a world's fair. The "spaceship" part has a restaurant, which turns slowly around.

 **Page 25** The Washington Monument honors George Washington. It stands 555 feet high. A law in Washington, D.C., says that no building there can ever be built higher than the monument.

 **Page 26** An engineer-in-training learns how to place blocks on her structure. What kind of tower can you build?

 **Page 27** Ironworkers erect the steel beams and columns that make up a building's skeleton. They also lay down the metal deck for the floors. Later, other workers will pour a concrete topping over the metal deck to finish the floor.

 **Page 28** Simon Rodia lived in the Watts neighborhood of Los Angeles. He built these towers right in his backyard. It took him 30 years. Broken tiles, bits of mirrors, and other odds and ends decorate his masterpiece. You can read *The Wonderful Towers of Watts*, by Patricia Zelver, to learn more.

 **Page 29** The Transamerica Pyramid was built in San Francisco in 1972. The 48 floors reach 853 feet in the sky.